D1309112

joy to the world

A CHRISTMAS SONGBOOK

National Gallery of Art

JOY to the world

A CHRISTMAS SONGBOOK

SOUTH COUNTRY LIBRARY
22 STATION ROAD
BELLPORT, NY 11713
JAN 0 7 1993

Hal Leonard Publishing Corporation

7777 West Bluemound Road P.O. Box 13819 Milwaukee, WI 53213

RIZZOLI
NEW YORK

First published in the United States of America in 1992 by
Rizzoli International Publications, Inc.
300 Park Avenue South, New York, New York 10010

Copyright © 1992
Rizzoli International Publications, Inc.

Music and lyrics copyright © 1992
Hal Leonard Publishing Corporation

Illustrations copyright © 1992
National Gallery of Art, Washington, D.C.

All rights reserved.
No part of this publication may be reproduced in any
manner whatsoever without permission in writing from Rizzoli
International Publications, Inc.

Designed by Nai Y. Chang

Printed and bound in Singapore

Library of Congress Cataloging-in-Publication Data

Joy to the world : a Christmas songbook / with an introduction
by William James Williams.
     1 score. For voice and piano.
     Words in English and other languages.
     Includes chord symbols.
     "Co-published with National Gallery of Art,
Washington, and Hal Leonard Publishing Corporation."
  ISBN 0-8478-1588-9 (hardback)
  —ISBN 0-7935-1428-2 (pbk.)
  1. Christmas music. 2. Songs with piano. 3. Carols.
4. Christmas in art. I. Williams, William James, 1942-
M1629.3.C5J7 1992   92-753969
                                     CIP
                                     M

Front cover illustration: Follower of Robert Campin
*Madonna and Child with Saints in the
Enclosed Garden* (c. 1440/1460) oil on oak
painted surface: 1.198 x 1.485 m (47¼ x 58½ in)
National Gallery of Art, Washington
Samuel H. Kress Collection 1959.9.3

Frontispiece: Belbello de Pavia, active 1448/1462
Annunciation to the Virgin (1450/1460)

CONTENTS

INTRODUCTION

This book encompasses a wide variety of familiar Christmas songs, ranging from Latin hymns through folk dances and American spirituals. The words and music are sometimes derived from generations of usage; other times, they are the creation of an individual genius such as Johann Sebastian Bach. Similarly, the paintings, drawings, prints, and sculpture reproduced from the National Gallery of Art include both rustic, home-made toys and sublime religious works, such as *The Small Cowper Madonna* by Raphael. These diverse songs and illustrations share a common bond of celebration, whether spiritual awe or secular joy.

"Christmas carols" is the phrase most often used to describe these songs, although to musicologists, the term carol has very specific meanings. Many works here are ballads which, like carols, narrate stories. Carols, however, alternate between repeated refrains called "burdens" and stanzas or verses of constant form but differing lyrics. They arose from various sources. Those with a lilting three-eight or six-eight time almost demand to be danced, and, indeed, they often originate from courtly or popular dance-songs. Other carols developed from dignified church liturgies and from spirited banquet entertainments.

Human expression in music, dance, drama, literature, and the visual arts is astonishingly complex and interrelated, especially when prompted by sacred occasions. The Bible accounts for merely seven events in Jesus' life as a baby and boy. In writing their Gospels, only two of the four Evangelists mention Christ's childhood at all, and their respective records do not overlap. The tax collector, Matthew, wrote about the wise men, while Luke, the physician, included only the shepherds. The desire to know more, to flesh out the life of Christ on earth, led to a marvelously rich biography for the young Jesus in both theological literature and popular legend. Composers, lyricists, and artists, in turn, embellished the Christmas story.

Even a date to celebrate Jesus' birth was not established until 354, when Bishop Liberius of Rome set the day at 25 December. This corresponded closely to the ancient Roman ritual of Saturn, a deity identified with the Greek god Cronos, whose name relates to the modern word chronology. The observances of these calendar gods sought a rebirth of the sun at the winter solstice around 22 December. Later in the fourth century, Saint Ambrose, the bishop of Milan, wrote the earliest known song dedicated to the Mass for Christ's birth.

As Christianity grew, new converts added their traditional customs to the notions of Christmas. The holly and pine trees once worshiped north of the Alps, for instance, came to symbolize the Christmas continuance of life because evergreens never fade, even in the depths of winter. Although the Book of Luke does not mention gifts or music at the Nativity, many charming folk tales have arisen about the peasants presenting livestock, fruit, and flowers, or of performing dances and songs with their drums and pipes. In Adriaen Isenbrant's painting *The Adoration of the Shepherds*, one peasant plays a bladder pipe. And, on the distant hilltop, other shepherds merrily circle a bonfire in a ring dance. Like the pagan Romans, the prehistoric peoples of northern Europe lit fires to rekindle the sun on the shortest day of the year. This coincidence helps explain the burning of Yule logs, just as the light from candles recalls the miraculous star in the Book of Matthew.

Other Christmas traditions grew from an interaction between the musical and visual arts. For instance, in medieval and Renaissance pictures, angels are usually depicted as boys and young men, much smaller in scale than the other figures in the compositions. Choirs at that time included many sweet-voiced youths who sang the soprano and alto parts. Therefore, the tiny angels in painting and sculpture accurately capture an element of daily life—the little boys in church choirs and liturgical dramas.

Those who lament the secular aspect of the modern holiday might be reminded that early medieval serfs often ignored Christmas church services in order to indulge in raucous revelries. Eventually, such festivities so offended the Puritans in seventeenth-century England and colonial New England that they banned public celebrations of Christmas altogether. Just as outright frivolity vanished, so too, the sterner aspects of the season have disappeared. Today, the threat of lumps of coal or willow switches in a child's shoe or stocking barely exists. The Child whose birth is commemorated came, after all, not to punish but to forgive.

The cultural popularization of the Christmas season during the last 200 years, though often decried, did much to revive fading religious customs. The singing of carols, for instance, had all but died out with the strict reforms of both the Catholic and Protestant churches during the late sixteenth and the seventeenth centuries. By the late eighteenth and early nineteenth centuries, however, the Christmas musical forms reappeared simultaneously with an increased invention among literary and visual artists. Many of the so-called carols from this period are, in fact, commercial songs.

Another instance of popularized tastes, Saint Nicholas was an early fourth-century bishop, long revered as a gift-giver and protector of children. His modern prominence in America, though, can be traced to *Knickerbocker's History of New York*, written by Washington Irving in 1809. This collection of Dutch colonial folk tales codified the image of a jolly old man who flies in a wagon to drop toys down chimneys. It took a while before the saint was transformed fully into Santa Claus. Clement Clarke Moore, a theologian, aided that development by writing *A Visit from Saint Nicholas*, best known by its opening line, "'Twas the night before Christmas." To guard his scholarly reputation, Moore published the poem anonymously in 1823; twenty-one years would pass before he would acknowledge authorship.

Similarly in 1843, Charles Dickens wrote a ghost story, a literary genre that amounted to a fad in contemporary England. Published serially in a popular magazine, *A Christmas Carol* gave us a character named Ebenezer Scrooge. This repulsive misanthrope is converted, by Yuletide love, into a repentant merrymaker. Scrooge quickly entered the world's imagination so thoroughly that even small children can identify him recast as the hero-villain of *How the Grinch Stole Christmas*, Dr. Seuss' doggerel verse of 1957. Another recent contribution to the season's warm-hearted sentiment is Gian Carlo Menotti's *Amahl and the Night Visitors*, an opera commissioned specifically for broadcast in 1951 by that most popular and commercial of media—television.

Christmas songs of this later twentieth-century period are not included in this collection, partly because sufficient time has not yet passed for them to be considered truly classics. How long that might take, no one can tell. Two centuries ago, the German tradition of decorating evergreens would have puzzled most Americans; yet, several songs in this book extol the Christmas tree. Only two generations ago, most people in the United States would have been equally perplexed by the now-familiar poinsettia from Mexico. Christmas, therefore, has been celebrated in a remarkable variety of both sacred and worldly customs, and its musical and visual expressions continue to be enriched.

Whether we observe solemn ritual or enjoy spirited gatherings, Christmas is a time for sharing with family, neighbor, and friend. The songs in this book are designed for sight-reading in churches, schools, and homes, or while caroling outdoors. The music is scored for voice and piano, and includes chord symbols for guitar and electric keyboard.

WILLIAM JAMES WILLIAMS

joy to the world

A CHRISTMAS SONGBOOK

ALL THROUGH THE NIGHT

Words by SIR HAROLD BOULTON
Traditional Welsh Melody

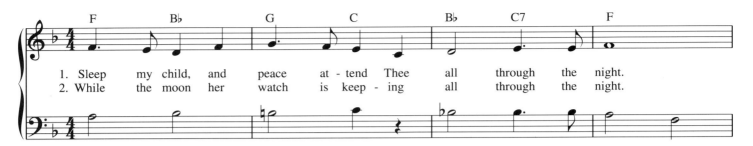

1. Sleep my child, and peace at-tend Thee all through the night.
2. While the moon her watch is keep-ing all through the night.

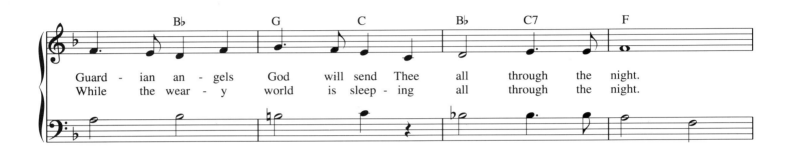

Guard-ian an-gels God will send Thee all through the night.
While the wear-y world is sleep-ing all through the night.

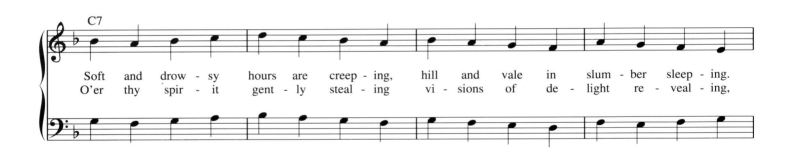

Soft and drow-sy hours are creep-ing, hill and vale in slum-ber sleep-ing.
O'er thy spir-it gent-ly steal-ing vi-sions of de-light re-veal-ing,

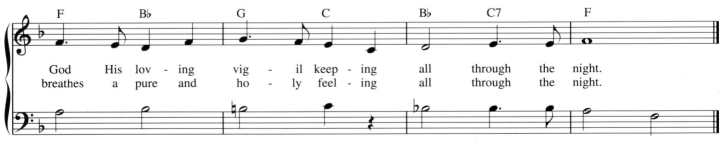

God His lov-ing vig-il keep-ing all through the night.
breathes a pure and ho-ly feel-ing all through the night.

Copyright © 1992 by HAL LEONARD PUBLISHING CORPORATION
International Copyright Secured   All Rights Reserved

Master of the Dominican Effigies, active 1336/1345
The Nativity with the Annunciation to the Shepherds (c. 1340)

13

After Annibale Fontana
The Adoration of the Shepherds (c. 1625/1675)

ANGELS FROM THE REALMS OF GLORY

Words by JAMES MONTGOMERY
Music by HENRY SMART

Firmly, not too slow

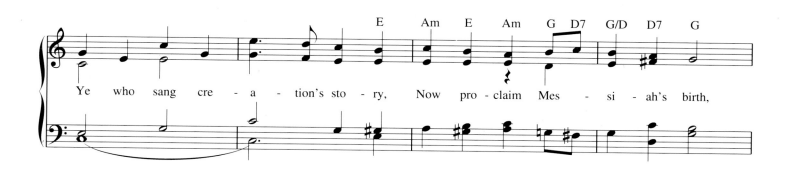

Copyright © 1992 by HAL LEONARD PUBLISHING CORPORATION
International Copyright Secured   All Rights Reserved

2. Shepherds in the fields abiding,
   Watching o'er your flocks by night,
   God with man is now residing
   Yonder shines the infant Light.
   Refrain

3. Sages, leave your contemplations
   Brighter visions beam afar,
   Seek the great Desire of nations
   Ye have seen His natal star.
   Refrain

ANGELS WE HAVE HEARD ON HIGH
(LES ANGES DANS NOS CAMPAGNES)

Traditional French Carol

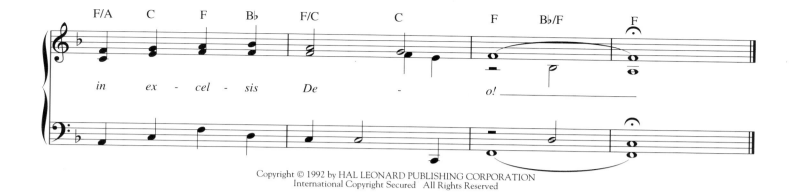

in ex - cel - sis De - o! _____

Copyright © 1992 by HAL LEONARD PUBLISHING CORPORATION
International Copyright Secured   All Rights Reserved

Juan de Flandes, active 1496–1519
The Nativity (c. 1508/1519)

1. *Les anges dans nos campagnes,*
   Ont entonné l'hymne des cieux,
   Et l'écho de nos montagnes
   Redit ce chant mélodieux:
   Refrain

2. *Bergers, pour qui cette fête!*
   Quel est l'objet de tous ces chants?
   Quel vainqueur, quelle conquête
   Mérite ces cris triomphants?
   Refrain

3. *Ils annoncent la naissance*
   Du libérateur d'Israël,
   Et, pleins de reconnaissance,
   Chantent en ce jour solennel:
   Refrain

4. *Cherchons tous l'heureux village*
   Qui l'a vu naître sous ses toits;
   Offrons-lui le tendre hommage
   Et de nos cœurs et de nos voix!
   Refrain

AWAY IN A MANGER

Music by JONATHAN E. SPILLMAN

1. A - way in a _____ man - ger, no crib for His bed, The
2. Be near me Lord _____ Je - sus I ask for Thee to stay, Close

lit - tle Lord Je - sus lay down His sweet head. The
by me Lord for - ev - er lay and down love His me I head. pray. The Bless

Martin Schongauer, c. 1450–1491
The Nativity (c. 1480/1490)

Copyright © 1992 by HAL LEONARD PUBLISHING CORPORATION
International Copyright Secured   All Rights Reserved

BELL CAROL
(CAROL OF THE BELLS)
Traditional Ukranian Carol

Ring, _____ silv - 'ry bells, sing _____

joy - ous bells! Strong - ly they chime, sound with a rhyme, Christ - mas is here,

wel - come the King! Hark! to the bells, hark! to the bells tell - ing us all

Je - sus is King! Ring! Ring! ____ bells. _____

Copyright © 1992 by HAL LEONARD PUBLISHING CORPORATION
International Copyright Secured   All Rights Reserved

Hans Bol, 1534–1593
Winter Landscape with Skaters (c. 1584/1586)

THE BOAR'S HEAD CAROL

Traditional English Carol

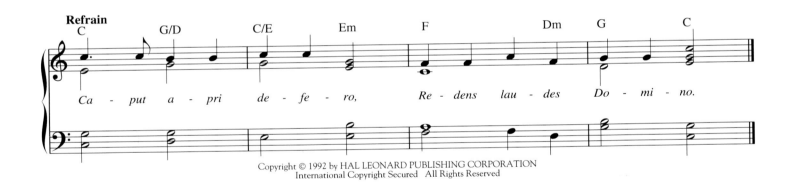

Copyright © 1992 by HAL LEONARD PUBLISHING CORPORATION
International Copyright Secured   All Rights Reserved

2. The boar's head, as I understand,
   Is the bravest dish in all the land,
   When thus bedeck'd with a gay garland.
   Let us *servire cantico*.
   Refrain

3. The boar's head that we bring here
   Betokeneth a prince without a peer
   Is born today to buy us dear;
   Nowell, nowell, nowell.
   Refrain

4. This boar's head we bring with song,
   In worship of Him that thus sprang
   Of a virgin to redress all wrong;
   Nowell, nowell, nowell.
   Refrain

5. Our steward hath provided this
   In honor of the King of Bliss,
   Which on this day to be served is,
   In Reginensi Atrio.
   Refrain

Lucas Cranach, the Elder, 1472–1553
Hunter on Horseback Hunting a Wild Boar (c. 1506)

BRING A TORCH, JEANNETTE, ISABELLA

(UN FLAMBEAU, JEANNETTE, ISABELLE)

Traditional Provençal Carol
Translation by E. CUTHBERT NUNN

G		Em		D		G		

Moth - er, Ah! ah! beau - ti - ful
slum - bers. Hush! hush! see how
sleep - ing. Hush! hush! see how how

D7   G

is Her Child! _____
fast He sleeps. _____
smiles in dreams. _____

Copyright © 1992 by HAL LEONARD PUBLISHING CORPORATION
International Copyright Secured   All Rights Reserved

1. *Un flambeau, Jeannette, Isabelle,*
   Un flambeau, courons au berceau!
   C'est Jésus, Bonnes gens du hameau,
   Le Christ est né, Marie appelle,
   Ah! ah! que la mère est belle,
   Ah! ah! ah! que l'Enfant est beau!

2. *C'est un tort quand l'Enfant sommeille,*
   C'est un tort de crier si fort.
   Taisez-vous, l'un et l'autre, d'abord!
   Au moindre bruit, Jesus s'éveille,
   Chut! chut! chut! Il dort à merveille,
   Chut! chut! chut! voyez comme Il dort!

3. *Doucement, dans l'étable close,*
   Doucement, venez un moment!
   Approchez, que Jésus est charmant!
   Comme Il est blanc, comme Il est rose!
   Do! do! do! que l'Enfant repose!
   Do! do! do! qu'Il rit en dormant!

Adriaen Isenbrant, active 1510–1551
The Adoration of the Shepherds
(probably 1520/1540)

CHRIST WAS BORN ON CHRISTMAS DAY

Moderately bright

1. Christ was born on Christ-mas day, wreath the hol-ly, twine the bay, *Christ - us na - tus ho - di - e* The Babe, the Son, the Ho - ly One of Ma - ry.

Copyright © 1992 by HAL LEONARD PUBLISHING CORPORATION
International Copyright Secured   All Rights Reserved

2. He is born to set us free,
   He is born our Lord to be,
   Ex Maria Virgine;
   The God, The Lord, by all adored forever.

3. Let the bright red berries glow,
   Everywhere in goodly show;
   Christus natus hodie;
   The Babe, the Son, the Holy One of Mary.

4. Christian men rejoice and sing,
   'Tis the birthday of a King,
   Ex Maria Virgine;
   The God, the Lord, by all adored forever.

Martin Schongauer, c. 1450–1491
The Nativity (c. 1470/1475)

THE COVENTRY CAROL

Words by ROBERT CROO
Traditional English Melody

Copyright © 1992 by HAL LEONARD PUBLISHING CORPORATION
International Copyright Secured   All Rights Reserved

2. O sisters too, how may we do,
   For to preserve this day.
   This poor youngling for whom we sing
   By, by, lully, lullay.

3. Herod the king, in his raging,
   Charged he hath this day.
   His men of might, in his own sight,
   All children young, to slay.

4. Then woe is me, poor child for thee!
   And ever mourn this day,
   For Thy parting neither say nor sing,
   By, by, lully, lullay.

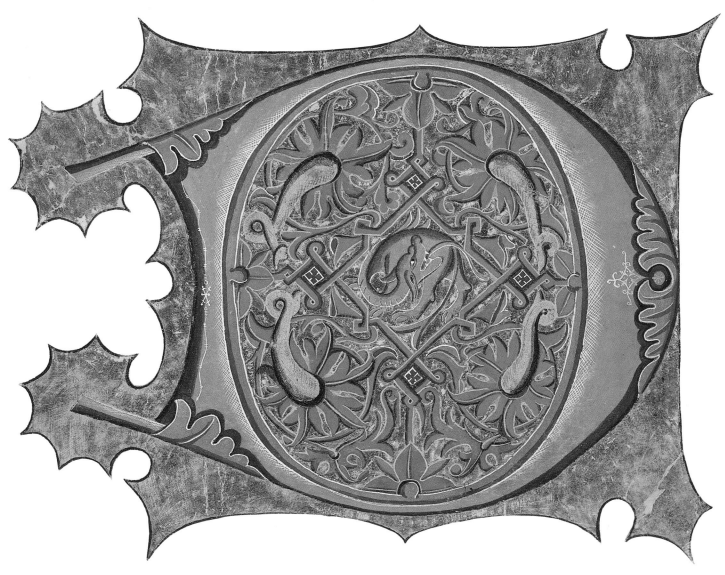

Master of the Cypresses, active 1434
Initial D (1430s)

DECK THE HALL

Traditional Welsh Carol

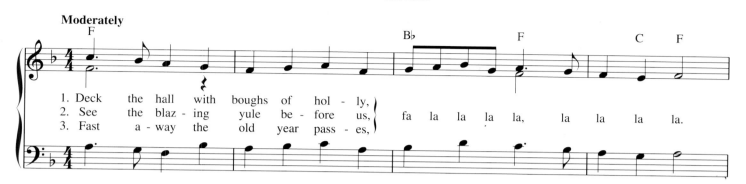

1. Deck the hall with boughs of hol - ly, fa la la la la, la la la la.
2. See the blaz - ing yule be - fore us,
3. Fast a - way the old year pass - es,

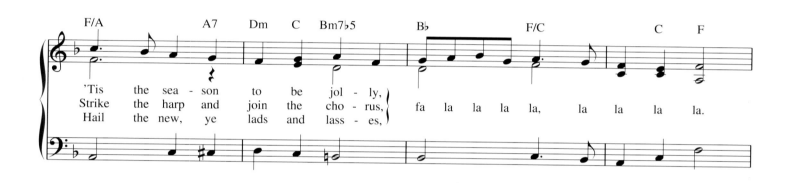

'Tis the sea - son to be jol - ly, fa la la la la, la la la la.
Strike the harp and join the cho - rus,
Hail the new, ye lads and lass - es,

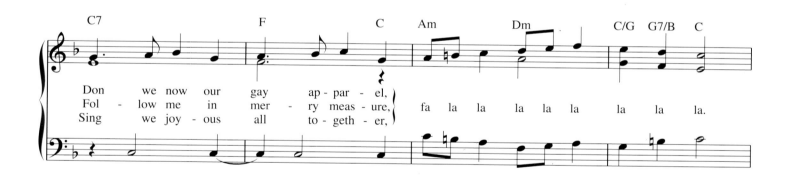

Don we now our gay ap - par - el, fa la la la la la la la la la.
Fol - low me in mer - ry meas - ure,
Sing we joy - ous all to - geth - er,

Troll the an - cient Yule - tide car - ol. Fa la la la la, la la la la.
While I tell of Yule - tide treas - ure.
Heed - less of the wind and weath - er.

Copyright © 1992 by HAL LEONARD PUBLISHING CORPORATION
International Copyright Secured   All Rights Reserved

Claude Monet, 1840–1926
Rouen Cathedral, West Façade, Sunlight (1894)

DING DONG, MERRILY ON HIGH

Traditional French Carol

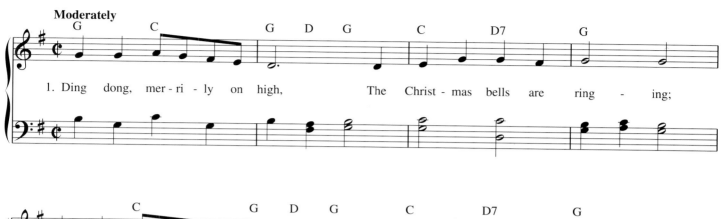

1. Ding dong, mer-ri-ly on high, The Christ-mas bells are ring - ing;

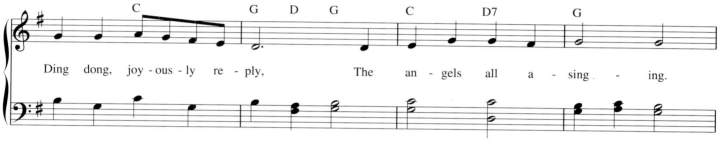

Ding dong, joy-ous-ly re-ply, The an-gels all a-sing - - ing.

Glo - - - -

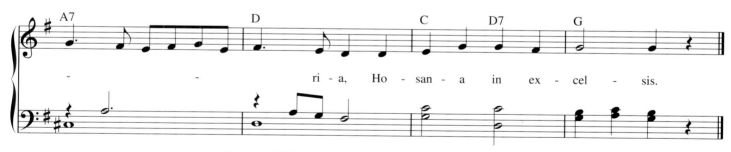

- - ri-a, Ho-san-a in ex-cel - sis.

Copyright © 1992 by HAL LEONARD PUBLISHING CORPORATION
International Copyright Secured   All Rights Reserved

2. Ding dong, carol all the bells,
   Ring out the Christmas story;
   Ding dong, sound the good nowells,
   God's Son has come in glory.
   Refrain

3. Praise Him! people far and near,
   And join the angels' singing.
   Ding dong, everywhere we hear
   The Christmas bells a-ringing.
   Refrain

2. Hear them ring this happy morn!
   Our God a gift has given;
   Ding dong, Jesus Christ is born!
   A precious Child from heaven.
   Refrain

THE FIRST NOWELL

Traditional English Carol

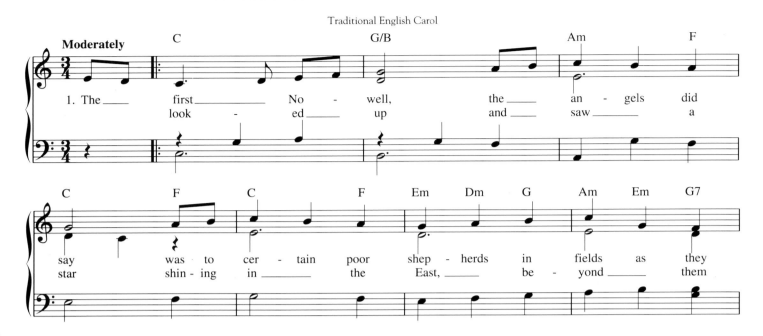

1. The _____ first _____ No - well, the _____ an - gels did
   look - ed _____ up and _____ saw _____ a

say _____ was to cer - tain poor shep - herds in fields as they
star shin - ing in _____ the East, _____ be - yond _____ them

Benedetto Montagna, c. 1480–1555 or 1558
Shepherd with a Platerspiel (c. 1500/1515)

3. And by the light of that same star
   Three wise men came from country far,
   To seek for a King was their intent,
   And to follow the star wherever it went.
   Refrain

4. This star drew nigh to the northwest;
   O'er Bethlehem it took its rest.
   And there it did both stop and stay,
   Right over the place where Jesus lay.
   Refrain

Copyright © 1992 by HAL LEONARD PUBLISHING CORPORATION
International Copyright Secured   All Rights Reserved

5. Then they did know assuredly
    Within that house, the King did lie
    One entered in then for to see
    And found the babe in poverty.
    Refrain

6. Then entered in those Wise Men three,
    Full reverently, upon bended knee,
    And offered there, in His presence,
    Their gold and myrrh and frankincense.
    Refrain

7. If we in our time do well
    We shall be free from death and hell
    For God hath prepared for us all
    A resting place in general.
    Refrain

33

THE FRIENDLY BEASTS

Traditional English Carol

Copyright © 1992 by HAL LEONARD PUBLISHING CORPORATION
International Copyright Secured   All Rights Reserved

3. "I," said the cow all white and red,
"I gave Him my manger for his bed;
I gave Him my hay to pillow His head."
"I," said the cow all white and red.

4. "I," said the sheep with the curly horn,
"I gave Him my wool for His blanket warm;
He wore my coat on Christmas morn."
"I," said the sheep with the curly horn.

5. "I," said the dove from the rafters high,
"I cooed Him to sleep that He would not cry;
We cooed Him to sleep, my mate and I."
"I," said the dove from the rafters high.

6. Thus every beast by some good spell,
In the stable dark was glad to tell
Of the gift he gave Emmanuel,
The gift he gave Emmanuel.

Edward Hicks, 1780–1849
Peaceable Kingdom (c. 1834)

FROM HEAVEN ABOVE
TO EARTH I COME
(VON HIMMEL HOCH, DA KOMM' ICH HER)

German Words by MARTIN LUTHER
English Translation by CATHERINE WINKWORTH
Melody Attributed to MARTIN LUTHER

Copyright © 1992 by HAL LEONARD PUBLISHING CORPORATION
International Copyright Secured   All Rights Reserved

1. *Vom Himmel hoch, da komm ich her,*
   Ich bring' euch gut neue Mär,
   Der guten Mär bring' ich so viel,
   Davon ich sing'n und sagen will.

2. *Euch ist ein Kindlein heut' gebor'n,*
   Von einer Jungfrau auserkor'n,
   Ein Kindelein so zart und fein,
   Das soll eu'r Freud' und Wonne sein.

3. *Lob, Ehr' sei Gott im höchsten Thron,*
   Der uns schenkt seinen ein'gen Sohn,
   Des freuen sich der Engel Schar
   Und singen uns solch neues Jahr.

FOOM, FOOM, FOOM
(FUM, FUM, FUM)

Traditional Catalonian Carol

Brightly

1. On De-cem-ber five and twen-ty, Foom, foom, foom! On De-cem-ber five and twen-ty,
2. Lit-tle birds from out the for-est, Foom, foom, foom! Lit-tle birds from out the for-est,
3. Lit-tle stars up in the heav-ens, Foom, foom, foom! Lit-tle stars up in the heav-ens,

Foom, foom, foom! For the love of us is giv'n the ho-ly In-fant, Son of Heav'n, of the
Foom, foom, foom! All the fledg-lings leave be-hind, and seek the in-fant Sav-ior kind. Come, and
Foom, foom, foom! If you see the ba-by cry, O, do not an-swer with a sigh! Rath-er,

Vir-gin, Jo-seph's bride, to all the earth good-will be tid-ing, Foom, foom, foom!
build a dow-ny nest to warm the love-ly ba-by bles-sed, Foom, foom, foom!
light-en up the sky with Heav'n's beams of ra-di-ant bright-ness, Foom, foom, foom!

Copyright © 1992 by HAL LEONARD PUBLISHING CORPORATION
International Copyright Secured   All Rights Reserved

Italian, 13th Century
The Nativity with Six Dominican Monks (c. 1275)

1. *¡Veinticinco de diciembre,*
   Fum, fum, fum!
   ¡Veinticinco de diciembre,
   Fum, fum, fum!
   Nacido ha por nuestro amor,
   El Niño Dios, el Niño, Dios;
   hoy de la virgen Maria
   En esta noche tan fría,
   ¡Fum, fum, fum!

2. *¡Pajaritos de los bosques,*
   Fum, fum, fum!
   ¡Pajaritos de los bosques,
   Fum, fum, fum!
   Vuestros hijos de coral
   Abandonad, abandonad,
   Y formad un muelle nido
   A Jesús recién nacido,
   ¡Fum, fum, fum!

3. *¡Estrellitas de los cielos,*
   Fum, fum, fum!
   ¡Estrellitas de los cielos,
   Fum, fum, fum!
   Que a Jesús miráis llorar
   Y no lloráis, y no lloráis,
   Alumbrad la noche oscura
   Con vuestra luz clara y pura,
   ¡Fum, fum, fum!

GLOUCESTERSHIRE WASSAIL

Traditional English Carol

Copyright © 1992 by HAL LEONARD PUBLISHING CORPORATION
International Copyright Secured   All Rights Reserved

David Teniers II, 1610–1690
Peasants Celebrating Twelfth Night (1635)

GOD REST YE MERRY, GENTLEMEN

Traditional English Carol

Copyright © 1992 by HAL LEONARD PUBLISHING CORPORATION
International Copyright Secured   All Rights Reserved

Andrea della Robbia,
1435–1525
*The Adoration of
the Child*
(after 1477)

3. The shepherds at those tidings
   Rejoicèd much in mind,
   And left their flocks a-feeding,
   In tempest, storm and wind,
   And went to Bethlehem straightway
   This blessèd babe to find:
   Refrain

4. But when to Bethlehem they came,
   Whereat this infant lay,
   They found him in a manger,
   Where oxen feed on hay;
   His mother Mary kneeling,
   Unto the Lord did pray:
   Refrain

GOOD KING WENCESLAS

Words by J.M. NEALE
Melody from *Piae Cantiones* (1582)

Copyright © 1992 by HAL LEONARD PUBLISHING CORPORATION
International Copyright Secured   All Rights Reserved

Master of the Cypresses, active 1434
Initial S with King David as Scribe (1430s)

2. "Hither page, and stand by me,
    If thou know'st it, telling,
    Yonder peasant, who is he?
    Where and what his dwelling?"
    "Sire, he lives a good league hence,
    Underneath the mountain;
    Right against the forest fence,
    By Saint Agnes' fountain."

3. "Bring me food, and bring me wine,
    Bring me pine logs hither;
    Thou and I will see him dine,
    When we bear them thither."
    Page and monarch forth they went,
    Forth they went together;
    Through the rude winds' wild lament:
    And the bitter weather.

4. "Sire, the night is darker now,
    And the wind blows stronger;
    Fails my heart, I know not how,
    I can go not longer."
    "Mark my footsteps, my good page,
    Tread thou in them boldly:
    Thou shalt find the winter's rage
    Freeze thy blood less coldly."

5. In his master's steps he trod,
    Where the snow lay dinted;
    Heat was in the very sod
    Which the saint had printed.
    Therefore, Christian men, be sure,
    Wealth or rank possessing,
    Ye who now will bless the poor,
    Shall yourselves find blessing.

GOOD CHRISTIAN MEN, REJOICE

Words by JOHN MASON NEALE
Traditional German Melody

Copyright © 1992 by HAL LEONARD PUBLISHING CORPORATION
International Copyright Secured   All Rights Reserved

Refrain
2. Now ye hear of endless bliss;
   Joy! Joy! Jesus Christ was born for this
   He hath ope'd the heav'nly doors,
   And man is blessed evermore.
   Christ was born for this!
   Christ was born for this!

Refrain
3. Now ye need not fear the grave;
   Peace! Peace! Jesus Christ was born to save!
   Calls you one and calls you all,
   To gain His everlasting hall.
   Christ was born to save!
   Christ was born to save!

HE IS BORN, THE HOLY CHILD

(IL EST NÉ, LE DIVIN ENFANT)

Traditional French Carol

Copyright © 1992 by HAL LEONARD PUBLISHING CORPORATION
International Copyright Secured   All Rights Reserved

Refrain
Il est né, le divin Enfant,
Jouez hautbois, résonnez musettes!
Il est né, le divin Enfant,
Chantons tous son avènement!

1. *Depuis plus de quatre mille ans,*
   Nous l'annoncaient les prophètes
   Depuis plus de quatre mille ans,
   Nous attendions cet heureux temps.
   Refrain

2. *Ah! Qu'il est beau, qu'il est charmant!*
   Que ses grâces sont parfaites!
   Ah! qu'il est beau, qu'il est charmant!
   Qu'il est doux ce Divin Enfant!
   Refrain

HARK! THE HERALD ANGELS SING

Words by CHARLES WESLEY and T. WHITEFIELD
Music by FELIX MENDELSSOHN

Copyright © 1992 by HAL LEONARD PUBLISHING CORPORATION
International Copyright Secured   All Rights Reserved

Gabriel Weather Vane (1840)
Index of American Design

2. Christ by highest heav'n adored,
   Christ, the everlasting Lord,
   Late in time behold him come
   Offspring of a virgin's womb:
   Veiled in flesh the God-head see,
   Hail the incarnate Deity!
   Pleased as man with man to dwell,
   Jesus, our Emmanuel.
   Refrain

3. Hail the heav'n-born Prince of Peace!
   Hail the Sun of Righteousness!
   Light and life to all He brings,
   Risen with healing in his wings;
   Mild he lays his glory by,
   Born that man no more may die,
   Born to raise the sons of earth,
   Born to give them second birth.
   Refrain

4. Come! Desire of nations, come!
   Fix in us Thy humble home:
   Rise, the woman's conqu'ring seed,
   Bruise in us the serpent's head;
   Adam's likeness now efface,
   Stamp Thine image in its place:
   Second Adam from above,
   Reinstate us in Thy love.
   Refrain

HERE WE COME A-WASSAILING

Traditional Yorkshire Carol

Copyright © 1992 by HAL LEONARD PUBLISHING CORPORATION
International Copyright Secured   All Rights Reserved

Jan Steen, 1626–1679
The Dancing Couple (1663)

3. We have got a little purse
   Of stretching leather skin;
   We want a little money,
   To line it well within:
   Refrain

4. God bless the master of this house,
   Likewise the mistress too;
   And all the little children,
   That 'round the table go:
   Refrain

5. Good master and good mistress,
   While you're sitting by the fire,
   Pray think of us poor children
   Who wander in the mire:
   Refrain

THE HOLY CHILD
(EL SANTO NIÑO)

Traditional Puerto Rican Carol

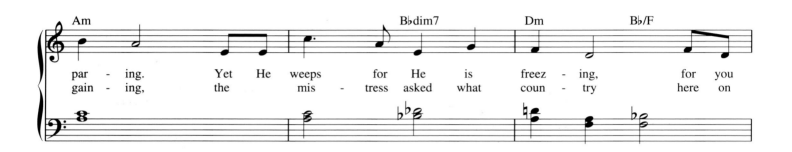

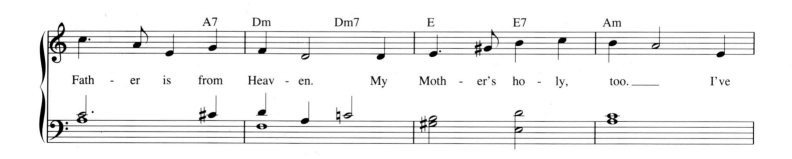

Copyright © 1992 by HAL LEONARD PUBLISHING CORPORATION
International Copyright Secured   All Rights Reserved

Raphael, 1483–1520
The Small Cowper Madonna (c. 1505)

1. *"Madre a la puerta hay un niño*
   Mas hermoso que el sol bello;
   Llorando muerte de frió,
   Y sin duda riene en cueras."

2. *Entra el niño y se calienta y*
   Después del calentado,
   Le pregunta la padrona
   De qué tierra es su reinado.

3. *"Mi padre es del cielo,*
   Mi madre también.
   Yo bajé a la tierra
   Para proceder!"

I HEARD THE BELLS ON CHRISTMAS DAY

Music by J. BAPTISTE CALKIN
Words by HENRY W. LONGFELLOW

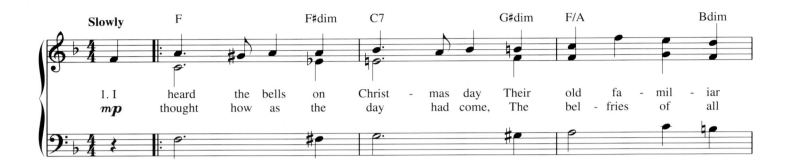

1. I heard the bells on Christ - mas day Their old fa - mil - iar
thought how as the day had come, The bel - fries of all

3. And in despair I bow'd my head:
   "There is no peace on earth," I said,
   "For hate is strong, and mocks the song
   Of peace on earth, good will to men."

4. Then pealed the bells more loud and deep:
   "God is not dead, nor doth He sleep;
   The wrong shall fail, the right prevail,
   With peace on earth, good will to men."

5. Till, ringing, singing on its way,
   The world revolved from night to day,
   A voice, a chime, a chant sublime,
   Of peace on earth, good will to men!

Hendrick Avercamp, 1585–1634
A Scene on the Ice (c. 1625)

car - ols play And mild and sweet the words re - peat, Of
Christ - en - dom Had roll'd a - long th'un - bro - ken song Of

peace on earth good will to men. 2. I will to men.
peace on earth good will to men. 3. And *rit.* to men.

1.-4.
Last time

Copyright © 1992 by HAL LEONARD PUBLISHING CORPORATION
International Copyright Secured   All Rights Reserved

I SAW THREE SHIPS

Traditional English Carol

Copyright © 1992 by HAL LEONARD PUBLISHING CORPORATION
International Copyright Secured   All Rights Reserved

Robert Salmon, 1775–c. 1845
The Ship "Favorite" Maneuvering off Greenock (1819)

3. Our Savior Christ and His lady.
   On Christmas Day, on Christmas Day;
   Our Savior Christ and His lady,
   On Christmas Day in the morning.

4. Pray, whither sailed those ships all three?
   On Christmas Day, on Christmas Day;
   Pray, whither sailed those ships all three?
   On Christmas Day in the morning.

5. O, they sailed in to Bethlehem,
   On Christmas Day, on Christmas Day;
   O, they sailed in to Bethlehem,
   On Christmas Day in the morning.

6. And all the bells on earth shall ring,
   On Christmas Day, on Christmas Day;
   And all the bells on earth shall ring,
   On Christmas Day in the morning.

7. And all the angels in Heav'n shall sing,
   On Christmas Day, on Christmas Day;
   And all the angels in Heav'n shall sing,
   On Christmas Day in the morning.

8. And all the souls on earth shall sing,
   On Christmas Day, on Christmas day;
   And all the souls on earth shall sing,
   On Christmas Day in the morning.

9. Then let us all rejoice again!
   On Christmas Day, on Christmas Day;
   Then let us all rejoice again!
   On Christmas Day in the morning.

IT CAME UPON A MIDNIGHT CLEAR

Music by RICHARD S. WILLIS
Words by EDMUND H. SEARS

heaven's ___ all gra - cious King." _____ The

world in sol - emn still - ness lay, To

hear the an - gels sing. _____
rit.

Copyright © 1992 by HAL LEONARD PUBLISHING CORPORATION
International Copyright Secured   All Rights Reserved

2. Still through the cloven skies they come,
   With peaceful wings unfurled;
   And still their heavenly music floats
   O'er all the weary world;
   Above its sad and lowly plains
   They bend on hovering wing:
   And ever o'er its Babel sounds
   The blessed angels sing.

3. Yet with the woes of sin and strife
   The world has suffered long;
   Beneath the angel-strain have rolled
   Two thousand years of wrong:
   And man, at war with man, hears not
   The love song which they bring:
   O hush the noise, ye men of strife.
   And hear the angels sing!

4. For lo! the days are hastening on,
   By prophet-bards foretold,
   When, with the ever-circling years,
   Comes round the age of gold:
   When peace shall over all the earth
   Its ancient splendors fling,
   And the whole world send back the song
   Which now the angels sing.

Lorenzo Lotto, c. 1480–1556
The Nativity (1523)

Thomas Cole, 1801–1848
The Voyage of Life: Youth (1842)

JESU, JOY OF MAN'S DESIRING

Traditional German Hymn Tune
Setting by J.S. BACH

1. Je

Copyright © 1992 by HAL LEONARD PUBLISHING CORPORATION
International Copyright Secured   All Rights Reserved

2. Jesu, joy of man's desiring,
Holy wisdom, love most bright,
Drawn by Thee our souls aspiring,
Soar to uncreated light.

3. Word of God our flesh that fashioned,
With the fire of life impassioned.
Striving still to truth unknown,
Soaring dying round Thy throne.

4. Through the way where hope is guiding,
Hark, peaceful music rings,
Where the flock in Thee confiding,
Drink of joy from deathless springs.

5. Theirs is beauty's fairest pleasure,
Theirs is wisdom's holiest treasure.
Thou dost ever lead Thine own,
In the love of joys unknown.

JINGLE BELLS

Words and Music by J. PIERPONT

Oh what fun it is to ride in a one horse o - pen sleigh! _____

Jin - gle bells, jin - gle bells, jin - gle all the way. Oh what fun it

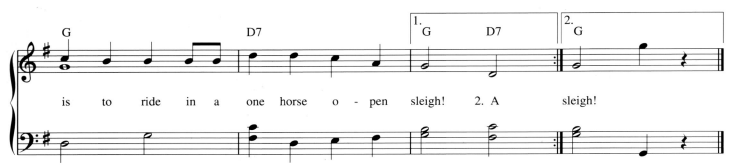

is to ride in a one horse o - pen sleigh! 2. A sleigh!

Copyright © 1992 by HAL LEONARD PUBLISHING CORPORATION
International Copyright Secured   All Rights Reserved

3. Now the ground is white so go it while you're young.
Take the girls tonight and sing this sleighing song.
Just get a bob-tail bay, two-forty for his speed,
Then hitch him to an open sleigh and crack!
    You'll take the lead! Oh!
    Refrain

Frances Flora Bond Palmer, c. 1812–1876
American Winter Scenes: Morning (published 1854)

JOLLY OLD ST. NICHOLAS

Traditional American Carol

Brightly

1. Jol - ly Old St. Ni - cho - las, Lean your ear this way!

Don't you tell a sin - gle soul What I'm going to say;

Chirst - mas Eve is com - ing soon; Now you dear old man,

Whis - per what you'll bring to me; Tell me if you can.

Copyright © 1992 by HAL LEONARD PUBLISHING CORPORATION
International Copyright Secured   All Rights Reserved

2. When the clock is striking twelve,
   When I'm fast asleep,
   Down the chimney broad and black,
   With your pack you'll creep;
   All the stockings you will find
   Hanging in a row;
   Mine will be the shortest one,
   You'll be sure to know.

3. Johnny wants a pair of skates;
   Susy wants a sled;
   Nellie wants a picture book
   Yellow, blue, and red;
   Now I think I'll leave to you
   What to give the rest;
   Choose for me, dear Santa Claus,
   You will know the best.

Toy Bank: Santa Claus (c. 1940)
Index of American Design

JOY TO THE WORLD

Music by G.F. HANDEL
Words by ISAAC WATTS

Copyright © 1992 by HAL LEONARD PUBLISHING CORPORATION
International Copyright Secured   All Rights Reserved

German, 15th Century
Madonna in a Closed Garden (1450/1470)

66

LO, HOW A ROSE E'ER BLOOMING
(ES IST EIN' ROS' ENTSPRUNGEN)

Traditional German Carol

Copyright © 1992 by HAL LEONARD PUBLISHING CORPORATION
International Copyright Secured   All Rights Reserved

1. *Es ist ein' Ros' entsprungen*
   Aus einer Wurzel zart,
   Wie uns die Alten sungen,
   Aus Jesse kam die Art,
   Und hat ein Blümlein bracht
   Mitten im kalten Winter,
   Wohl zu der halben Nacht.

2. *Das Röslein, das ich meine,*
   Davon Isaias sagt,
   Hat uns gebracht alleine
   Marie, die reine Magd.
   Aus Gottes ew'gen Rat
   Hat sie ein Kind geboren,
   Wohl zu der halben Nacht.

3. *Das Blümelein, so kleine,*
   Das duftet uns so süss;
   Mit seinem hellen Scheine
   Vertreibt's die Finsternis;
   Wahr' Mensch un wahrer Gott,
   Hilft uns aus allen Leiden,
   Rettet von Sünd' und Tod.

Gerard David, c. 1460–1523
The Rest on the Flight into Egypt (c. 1510)

MARY HAD A BABY

Traditional Spiritual

Moderately

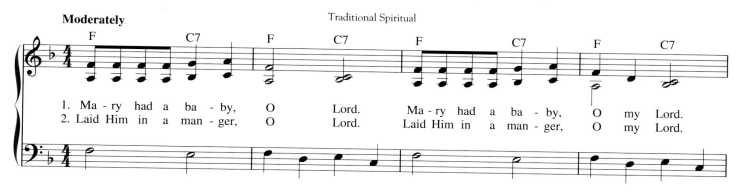

1. Ma - ry had a ba - by, O Lord. Ma - ry had a ba - by, O my Lord.
2. Laid Him in a man - ger, O Lord. Laid Him in a man - ger, O my Lord.

Ma - ry had a ba - by,
Laid Him in a man - ger, } O Lord. The peo - ple keep - a - com - in' and the train done gone.

Copyright © 1992 by HAL LEONARD PUBLISHING CORPORATION
International Copyright Secured   All Rights Reserved

3. Shepherds came to see Him, O Lord.
   Shepherds came to see Him, O my Lord.
   Shepherds came to see Him, O Lord.
   The people keep a comin' and the train done gone.

4. Named Him King Jesus, O Lord.
   Named Him King Jesus, O my Lord.
   Named Him King Jesus, O Lord.
   The people keep a comin' and the train done gone.

MARCH OF THE TOYS

Written by VICTOR HERBERT

Toy Locomotive (1850–1875)
Index of American Design

Copyright © 1992 by HAL LEONARD PUBLISHING CORPORATION
International Copyright Secured   All Rights Reserved

NOËL! NOËL!

Traditional French Carol

Copyright © 1992 by HAL LEONARD PUBLISHING CORPORATION
International Copyright Secured   All Rights Reserved

O CHRISTMAS TREE

(O TANNENBAUM)

Traditional German Carol

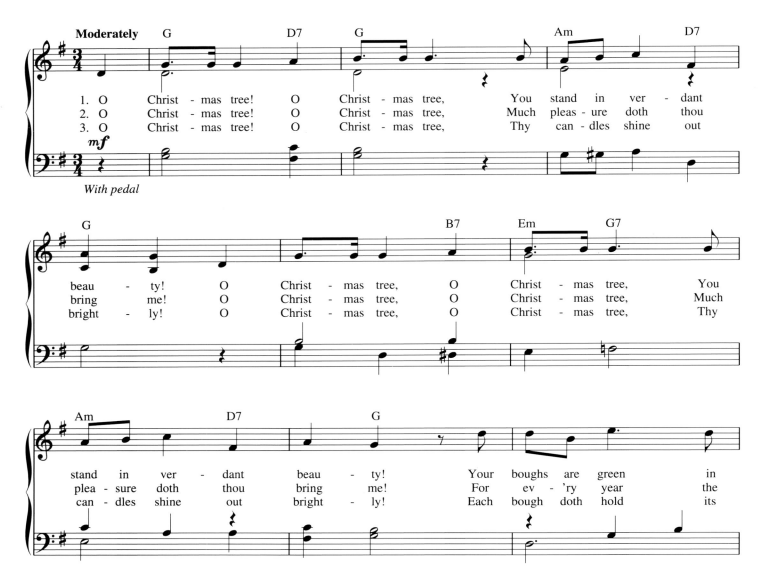

1. O Christ - mas tree! O Christ - mas tree, You stand in ver - dant
2. O Christ - mas tree! O Christ - mas tree, Much pleas - ure doth thou
3. O Christ - mas tree! O Christ - mas tree, Thy can - dles shine out

beau - ty! O Christ - mas tree, O Christ - mas tree, You
bring me! O Christ - mas tree, O Christ - mas tree, Much
bright - ly! O Christ - mas tree, O Christ - mas tree, Thy

stand in ver - dant beau - ty! Your boughs are green in
plea - sure doth thou bring me! For ev - 'ry year the
can - dles shine out bright - ly! Each bough doth hold its

sum - mer's glow, And do not fade in win - ter's snow. O
Christ - mas tree, Brings to us all both joy and glee. O
ti - ny light, That makes each toy to spar - kle bright. O

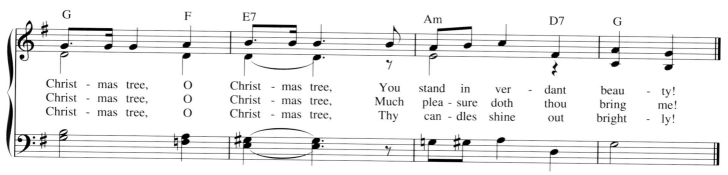

Christ - mas tree, O Christ - mas tree, You stand in ver - dant beau - ty!
Christ - mas tree, O Christ - mas tree, Much plea - sure doth thou bring me!
Christ - mas tree, O Christ - mas tree, Thy can - dles shine out bright - ly!

Copyright © 1992 by HAL LEONARD PUBLISHING CORPORATION
International Copyright Secured   All Rights Reserved

1. *O Tannenbaum, O Tannenbaum,*
   Wie treu sind deine Blätter!
   O Tannenbaum, O Tannenbaum,
   Wie treu sind deine Blätter!
   Du grünst nicht nur zur Sommerzeit,
   Nein, auch im Winter, wenn es schneit.
   O Tannenbaum, O Tannenbaum,
   Wie treu sind deine Blätter!

2. *O Tannenbaum, O Tannenbaum,*
   Du kannst mir sehr gefallen!
   O Tannenbaum, O Tannenbaum,
   Du kannst mir sehr gefallen!
   Wie oft hat mich zur Weihnachtszeit
   Ein Baum von dir mich hoch erfreut!
   O Tannenbaum, O Tannenbaum,
   Du kannst mir sehr gefallen!

3. *O Tannenbaum, O Tannenbaum,*
   Dein Kleid soll mich was lehren!
   O Tannenbaum, O Tannenbaum,
   Dein Kleid soll mich was lehren!
   Die Hoffnung und Beständigkeit
   Gibt Trost und Kraft zu aller Zeit.
   O Tannenbaum, O Tannenbaum,
   Dein Kleid soll mich was lehren!

O COME ALL YE FAITHFUL
(ADESTE FIDELES)

Words and Music by J.F. WADE

come,   let   us   a -   dore   Him,____   Christ _____   the   Lord!

Copyright © 1992 by HAL LEONARD PUBLISHING CORPORATION
International Copyright Secured   All Rights Reserved

Botticelli, 1444/1445–1510
The Adoration of the Magi (early 1480s)

1. *Adeste fideles, læti triumphantes,*
   Venite, venite in Bethlehem!
   Natum videte Regem angelorum:

   Refrain
   Venite adoremus, venite adoremus,
   Venite adoremus, Dominum.

2. *Cantet nunc Io! chorus angelorum;*
   Cantet nunc aula cælestium:
   Gloria, gloria, in excelsis Deo:
   Refrain

3. *Ergo qui natus die hodierna,*
   Jesu, tibi sit gloria!
   Patris æterni Verbum caro factum:
   Refrain

Hendrik Goltzius, 1558–1617
*The Holy Family with Saint Elizabeth and Saint
John the Baptist* (1595)

O COME, LITTLE CHILDREN
(IHR KINDERLEIN, KOMMET)

Words by CHRISTOPH VON SCHMID
Music by J.A.P. SCHULZ

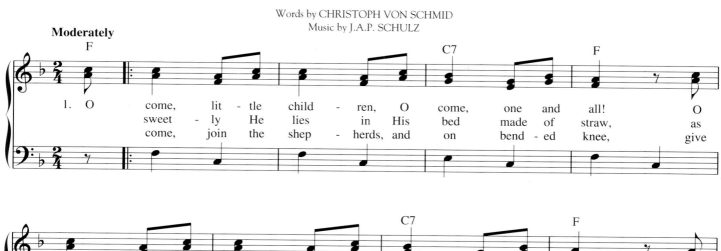

1. O come, lit-tle child-ren, O come, one and all!
sweet-ly He lies in His bed made of straw, as
come, join the shep-herds, and on bend-ed knee, give

come to the cra-dle in Beth-le-hem's stall! Come,
Mar-y and Jo-seph be-hold Him in awe! The
thanks to the Fath-er for Je-sus, our king. O

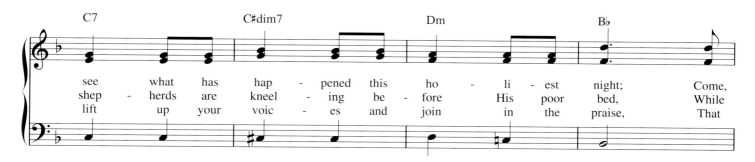

see what has hap-pened this ho-li-est night; Come,
shep-herds are kneel-ing be-fore His poor bed, While
lift up your voic-es and join His in the praise, That

gaze on the gift from the Fath-er of Might. 2. How
car-ol-ing an-gels are heard o-ver-head. 3. O
an-gels from Heav'n to the Fath-er now raise.

Copyright © 1992 by HAL LEONARD PUBLISHING CORPORATION
International Copyright Secured All Rights Reserved

1. *Ihr Kinderlein, kommet, O kommet doch all!*
   Zur Krippe her kommet, in Bethlehems stall!
   Und seht, was in dieser hochheiligen Nacht
   Der Vater in Himmel für Freude uns Macht.

2. *Da liegt es, ihr Kinder, auf Heu und auf Stroh,*
   Maria und Joseph betrachten es froh,
   Der edlichen Hirten knie'n betend davor,
   Hoch oben schwebt jubelnd der Engelein Chor.

3. *O beugt, wie die Hirten, anbetend die Knie,*
   Erhebet die Händlein und danket wie sie!
   Stimmt freudig, ihr Kinder, wer sollt' ich nicht freu'n?
   Stimmt freudig zum Jubel der Engel mit ein.

O COME, O COME, EMMANUEL

Traditional Latin Carol

Copyright © 1992 by HAL LEONARD PUBLISHING CORPORATION
International Copyright Secured   All Rights Reserved

1. Veni, veni Emmanuel,
   Captivum solve Israel,
   Qui gemit in exilio,
   Privatus Dei filio.
   Refrain

2. Veni, veni O Oriens,
   Solare nos adveniens:
   Noctis despelle nebulas,
   Dirasque noctis tenebras.

3. Veni, clavis Davidica,
   Regna reclude caelica,
   Fac iter tutum superum,
   Et claude vias inferum.
   Refrain

Refrain

Gaude, Gaude Emmanuel,
Nascetur pro te Israel.

O HOLY NIGHT
(CANTIQUE DE NOËL)

French Words by CAPPEAU de ROQUEMAURE
English Words by D.S. DWIGHT
Music by ADOLPHE ADAM

Copyright © 1992 by HAL LEONARD PUBLISHING CORPORATION
International Copyright Secured   All Rights Reserved

Fra Angelico, c. 1400–1455
and Fra Filippo Lippi, c. 1406–1469
The Adoration of the Magi (c. 1445)

1. *Minuit, Chrétiens, c'est l'heure solennelle*
   Où l'homme Dieu descendit jusqu'à nous,
   Pour effacer la tache originelle,
   Et de son Père arrêter le courroux,
   Le monde entier tressaille d'espérance,
   A cette nuit qui lui donne un Sauveur.
   Peuple à genoux, attends ta délivrance.
   Noël! Noël! voici le Rédempteur!
   Noël! Noël! voici le Rédempteur!

2. *De notre foi que la lumière ardente*
   Nous guide tous au berceau de l'enfant,
   Comme autrefois une étoile brillante
   Y conduisit les chefs de l'Orient.
   Le Roi de rois naît dans une humble crèche;
   Puissants du jour, fiers de votre grandeur.
   A votre orgueil c'est de la qu'un Dieu prêche.
   Courbez vos fronts devant le Rédempteur!
   Courbez vos fronts devant le Rédempteur!

3. *Le Rédempteur a brisé toute entrave,*
   La terre est libre et le ciel est ouvert;
   Il voit un frère où n'était qu'un esclave;
   L'amour unit ceux qu'enchaînait le fer
   Qui lui dira notre reconnaissance?
   C'est pour nous tous qu'il naît, qu'il
      souffre et meurt.
   Peuple, debout, chante ta délivrance.
   Noël, Noël, chantons le Rédempteur!
   Noël, Noël, chantons le Rédempteur!

O HOW JOYFULLY

(O DU FRÖHLICHE)

German Words by JOHANNES FALK
Traditional Latin Melody

Copyright © 1992 by HAL LEONARD PUBLISHING CORPORATION
International Copyright Secured   All Rights Reserved

Refrain

O du fröhliche, O du selige,
gnadenbringende Weihnachtszeit!

1. *Welt ging verloren,*
   Christ ist geboren:
   Freue, freue dich,
   O Christenheit!

Refrain

2. *Christ ist erschienen,*
   Uns zu versühnen:
   Freue, freue dich,
   O Christenheit!

Refrain

3. *Himmlische Heere*
   Jauchzen dir Ehre:
   Freue, freue dich,
   O Christenheit!

ONCE IN ROYAL DAVID'S CITY

Words by CECIL F. ALEXANDER
Music by HENRY F. GAUNTLET

Not too fast

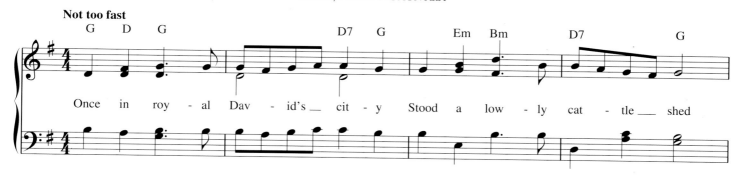

Once in roy-al Dav-id's __ cit-y Stood a low-ly cat-tle __ shed

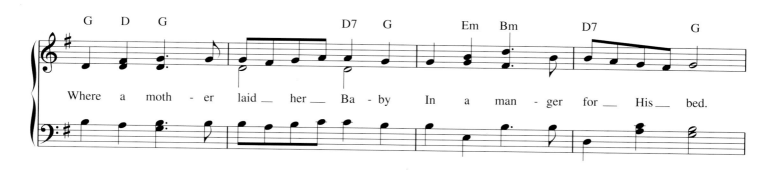

Where a moth-er laid __ her __ Ba-by In a man-ger for __ His __ bed.

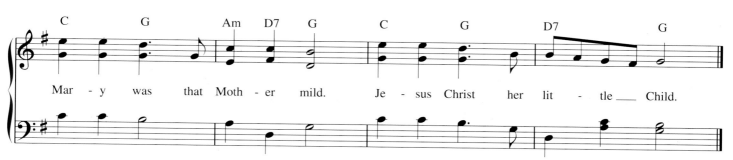

Mar-y was that Moth-er mild. Je-sus Christ her lit-tle __ Child.

Copyright © 1992 by HAL LEONARD PUBLISHING CORPORATION
International Copyright Secured   All Rights Reserved

2. He came down to earth from heaven,
Who is God and Lord of all,
And His shelter was a stable,
And His cradle was a stall.
With the poor and mean and lowly,
Lived on earth our Savior holy.
Refrain

3. And our eyes at last shall see Him,
Through His own redeeming love,
For that child so dear and gentle
Is our Lord in heaven above.
And He leads His children on
To the place where He is gone.
Refrain

O LITTLE TOWN OF BETHLEHEM

Words by PHILLIPS BROOKS
Music by LEWIS H. REDNER

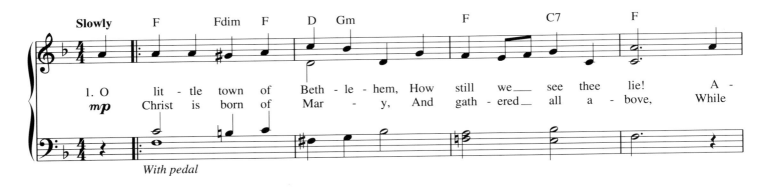

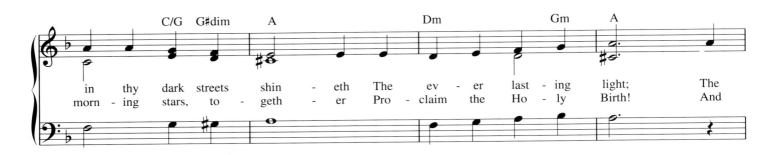

Copyright © 1992 by HAL LEONARD PUBLISHING CORPORATION
International Copyright Secured   All Rights Reserved

3. How silently, how silently the wondrous gift is given!
   So God imparts to human hearts the blessings of His heaven.
   No ear may hear His coming, but in this world of sin,
   Where meek souls will receive Him still,
   The dear Christ enters in.

4. O holy Child of Bethlehem! Descend to us we pray;
   Cast out our sin and enter in, be born in us today.
   We hear the Christmas angels the great glad tidings tell;
   O come to us, abide with us,
   Our Lord Emmanuel!

Benvenuto di Giovanni, 1436–c. 1518
The Adoration of the Magi (c. 1470)

PARADE OF THE WOODEN SOLDIERS

Music by LEON JESSEL

Copyright © 1992 by HAL LEONARD PUBLISHING CORPORATION
International Copyright Secured   All Rights Reserved

Duccio di Buoninsegna, c. 1255–1318
Center Panel: *The Nativity with the Prophets Isaiah and Ezekiel* (1308/1311)

REJOICE AND BE MERRY

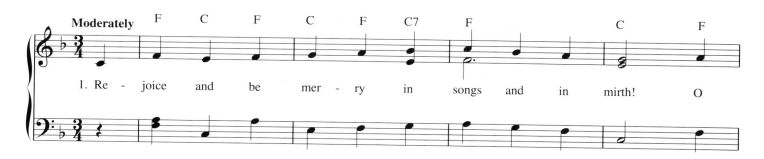

1. Re - joice and be mer - ry in songs and in mirth! O

praise our Re - deem - er, all mor - tals on earth! For

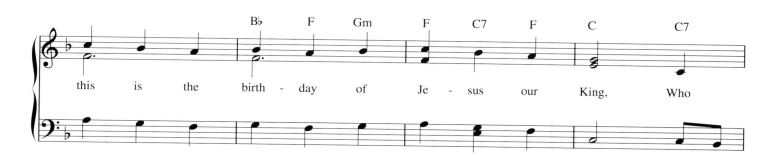

this is the birth - day of Je - sus our King, Who

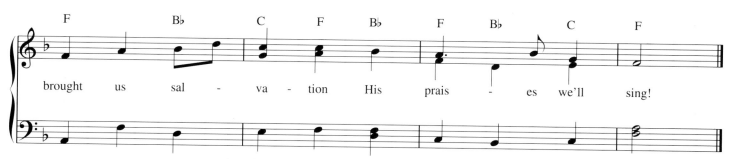

brought us sal - va - tion His prais - es we'll sing!

Copyright © 1992 by HAL LEONARD PUBLISHING CORPORATION
International Copyright Secured   All Rights Reserved

2. A heavenly vision appeared in the sky!
   Vast numbers of angels the shepherds did spy,
   Proclaiming the birthday of Jesus our King,
   Who brought us salvation His praises we'll sing!

3. Likewise a bright star in the sky did appear,
   Which led the wise men from the east to draw near:
   They found the Messiah, sweet Jesus our King,
   Who brought us slavation His praises we'll sing!

4. And when they were come, they their treasures unfold,
   And unto Him offered myrrh, incense and gold.
   So blessed forever be Jesus our King,
   Who brought us salvation His praises we'll sing!

Jacopo Tintoretto, 1518–1594
The Madonna of the Stars (second half 16th century)

THE ROCKING OF THE CHILD
(EL RORRO)

Traditional Mexican Carol

Copyright © 1992 by HAL LEONARD PUBLISHING CORPORATION
International Copyright Secured   All Rights Reserved

1. *A la ru-ru-ru, niño chiquito,*
   Duérmase ya mi Jesusito.
   Del elefante hasta el mosquito,
   Guarden silencio, no le hagan ruido.
   Refrain

2. *A la ru-ru-ru, niño chiquito,*
   Duérmase ya mi Jesusito.
   Coros celestiales, con su dulce acento,
   Cantan la ventura de este nacimiento.
   Refrain

3. *A la ru-ru-ru, niño chiquito,*
   Duérmase ya mi Jesusito.
   Noche venturosa, noche de alegría,
   Bendita la dulce, divina María.
   Refrain

SILENT NIGHT
(STILLE NACHT)

Music by FRANZ GRUBER
Words by JOSEPH MOHR
Translation by C.L. HUTCHINS

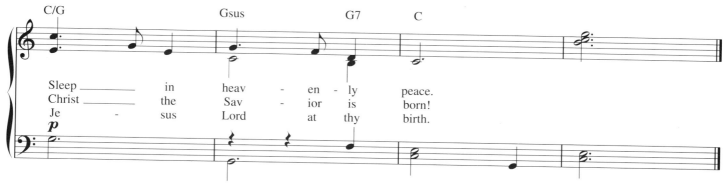

Sleep _____ in heav - en - ly peace.
Christ _____ the Sav - ior is born!
Je - sus Lord at thy birth.

p

Copyright © 1992 by HAL LEONARD PUBLISHING CORPORATION
International Copyright Secured   All Rights Reserved

1. *Stille Nacht, heilige Nacht!*
   Alles schläft, einsam wacht
   Nur des traute hochheilige Paar
   Holder Knabe im lockigen Haar
   Schlaf in himmlischer Ruh,
   Schlaf in himmlischer Ruh!

2. *Stille Nacht, heilige Nacht!*
   Hirten erst kundgemacht!
   Durch der Engel Halleluja
   Tönt es laut von fern und nah:
   Christ der Retter, ist da,
   Christ der Retter, ist da!

3. *Stille Nacht, heilige Nacht!*
   Gottes Sohn, O, wie lacht
   Lieb aus deinem göttlichen Mund,
   Da uns schlägt die rettende Stund,
   Christ, in deiner Geburt,
   Christ, in deiner Geburt.

Samuel Palmer, 1805–1881
The Sleeping Shepherd; Early Morning (1857)

SING WE NOW OF CHRISTMAS
(NOËL NOUVELET)

Traditional French Carol

Copyright © 1992 by HAL LEONARD PUBLISHING CORPORATION
International Copyright Secured   All Rights Reserved

2. When I woke this mornin' darkness still filled the sky
   Yet through my window a tree in bloom did I spy
   From which there sprang a marvelous flower
   Sing we now of Christmas, sing we here Noël.

3. My heart leapt for joy at the sight of this new tree.
   For its beauty shone forth as brilliantly
   As the sun that rises in the East.
   Sing we now of Christmas, sing we here Noël.

4. A lark sang to the shepherds when they heard it say;
   "Go now to Bethlehem, go without delay.
   There in a stable you will find a newborn Lamb."
   Sing we now of Christmas, sing we here Noël.

5. In that ancient village Joseph watch'd with Mary
   The oxen and the ass; the small sleeping baby.
   No cradle for the Babe, just a bed of straw.
   Sing we now of Christmas, sing we here Noël.

1. *Noël nouvelet, Noël chantons ici,*
   Dévotes gens, crions à Dieu merci!
   Chantons Noël pour le Roi nouvelet
   Noël nouvelet, Noël chantons Noël.

2. *Quand je m'éveillai et j'eus assez dormi,*
   Ouvris les yeux, vis un arbre fleuri,
   Dont il sortait un bouton merveillet.
   Noël nouvelet, Noël chantons Noël.

3. *Quand je le vis, mon cœur fut réjoui,*
   Car sa grand'beauté resplendissait en lui,
   Comme un soleil qui lève au matinet.
   Noël nouvelet, Noël chantons Noël.

4. *D'un oiselet après le chant ouïs,*
   Qui aux pasteurs disait: Partez d'ici;
   A Bethléem, trouvèrent l'agnelet.
   Noël nouvelet, Noël chantons Noël.

5. *En Bethléem Marie et Joseph vis,*
   L'âne et le bœuf; l'enfant couché au lit;
   La crèche était au lieu d'un bercelet.
   Noël nouvelet, Noël chantons Noël.

Agnolo Gaddi, active 1369–1396
The Coronation of the Virgin (detail)
(probably c. 1370)

SLEEP, SLEEP, PRECIOUS CHILD OF MINE
(DORMI, DORMI, O BEL BAMBIN)

Traditional Italian Carol

1. Sleep, sleep pre - cious Child of mine, King di - vine,
2. O my child why do you weep? My pre - cious love,

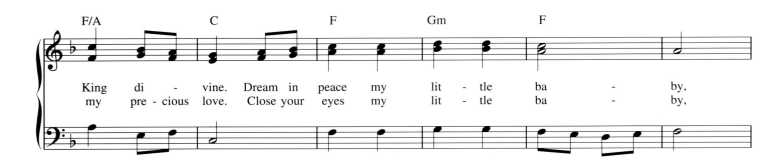

King di - vine. Dream in peace my lit - tle ba - by,
my pre - cious love. Close your eyes my lit - tle ba - by,

Martin Schongauer, c. 1450–1491
Madonna on the Crescent (c. 1470)

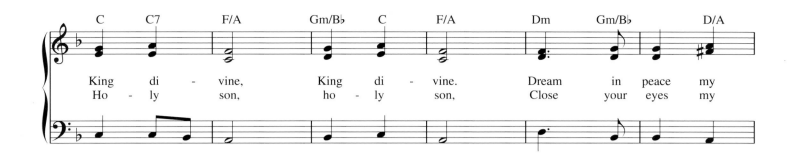

King di - vine, King di - vine. Dream in peace my
Ho - ly son, ho - ly son, Close your eyes my

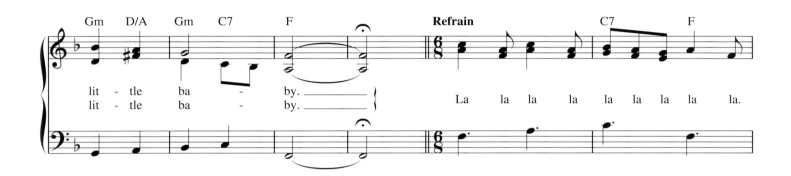

lit - tle ba - by. _____
lit - tle ba - by. _____

Refrain

La la la la la la la la la la.

La la la la la la la la. La la la la la la la la la. La la la la

la la la la. Fa la la, la la la, fa la la, la la la. Fa la la, la la la, fa la la, la.

Copyright © 1992 by HAL LEONARD PUBLISHING CORPORATION
International Copyright Secured   All Rights Reserved

1. *Dormi, dormi, o bel Bambin,*
   Rè divin, Rè divin,
   Fa la nanna, o fantolino.
   Rè divin, Rè divin.
   Fa la nanna, o fantolino.
   Refrain

2. *Perche piangi, o mio tresor?*
   Dolce amor, dolce amor!
   Fa la nanna, a caro figlio,
   Tanto bel, tanto bel,
   Fa la nanna, o caro figlio.
   Refrain

SLEEP, THOU LITTLE CHILD
(ENTRE LE BOEUF ET L'ÂNE GRIS)

Traditional French Carol

Copyright © 1992 by HAL LEONARD PUBLISHING CORPORATION
International Copyright Secured   All Rights Reserved

1. *Entre le boeuf et l'âne gris*
   Dort, dort, dort le petit Fils:

Refrain
   Mille anges divins,
   Mille Séraphins
   Volent àlentour
   De ce grand Dieu d'amour.

2. *Entre les roses et les lis,*
   Dort, dort, dort le petit Fils
   Refrain

3. *Entre les pastoureaux jolis,*
   Dort, dort, dort le petit Fils;
   Refrain

4. *En ce beau jour si solennel*
   Dort, dort, dort l'Emmanuel;
   Refrain

THE SNOW LAY ON THE GROUND

Traditional Irish Carol

Moderately Slow

Copyright © 1992 by HAL LEONARD PUBLISHING CORPORATION
International Copyright Secured   All Rights Reserved

TOYLAND

Words by GLEN MacDONOUGH
Music by VICTOR HERBERT

Doll (1867)

Carousel Reindeer (c. 1890)

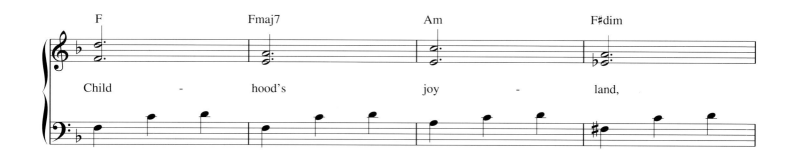

Child - hood's joy - land,

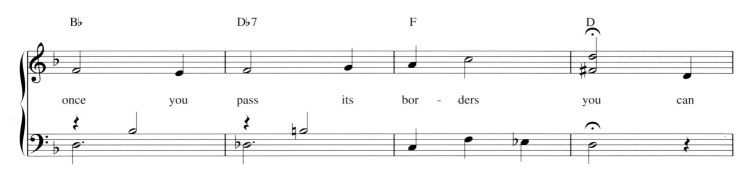

mys - tic mer - ry joy - land,

once you pass its bor - ders you can

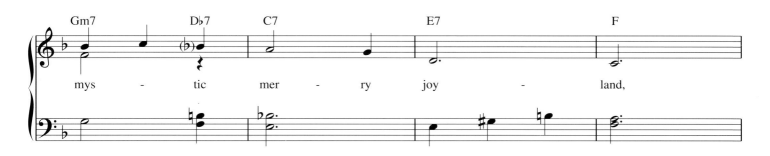

nev - er re - turn a - gain.

rit.

Copyright © 1992 by HAL LEONARD PUBLISHING CORPORATION
International Copyright Secured   All Rights Reserved

Top (c. 1830)

Toy Horse (c. 1830)
All from the Index of American Design

Charles V. Bond, c. 1825–in or after 1864
Still Life: Fruit, Bird, and Dwarf Pear Tree (1856)

THE TWELVE DAYS OF CHRISTMAS

Traditional English Carol

Copyright © 1992 by HAL LEONARD PUBLISHING CORPORATION
International Copyright Secured   All Rights Reserved

Seven swans a-swimming
Eight maids a-milking
Nine ladies dancing

Ten lords a-leaping
Eleven pipers piping
Twelve drummers drumming

UP ON THE HOUSETOP

Words and Music by B.R. HANDY

1. Up on the house-top reindeer pause, out jumps good old Santa Claus;
2. First comes the stocking of little Nell, oh, dear Santa fill it well;
3. Next comes the stocking of little Will, oh, just see what a glorious fill!

down thru the chimney with lots of toys, all for the little ones, Christmas joys.
give her a dollie that laughs and cries, one that will open and shut her eyes.
Here is a hammer and lots of tacks, also a ball and a whip that cracks.

Ho, ho, ho! Who wouldn't go? Ho, ho, ho! Who wouldn't go?

Up on the house-top, click, click, click, down through the chimney with good Saint Nick.

Ho, ho, ho! Who wouldn't go? Ho, ho, ho! Who wouldn't go?

Up on the house-top, click, click, click, down through the chimney with good Saint Nick.

Copyright © 1992 by HAL LEONARD PUBLISHING CORPORATION
International Copyright Secured   All Rights Reserved

Santa Claus Print (1888)
Index of American Design

WE WISH YOU A MERRY CHRISTMAS

Traditional English Carol

Brightly

We wish you a mer-ry Christ-mas, we wish you a mer-ry Christ-mas, we

wish you a mer-ry Christ-mas and a hap-py New Year. Good

tid-ings we bring to you and your kin, good tid-ings for

Christ-mas and a hap-py New Year. We wish you a mer-ry

Chrsit-mas, we wish you a mer-ry Christ-mas, we wish you a mer-ry

Christ-mas and a hap-py New Year. Good Year.

Copyright © 1992 by HAL LEONARD PUBLISHING CORPORATION
International Copyright Secured   All Rights Reserved

WE THREE KINGS

Words and Music by JOHN H. HOPKINS

We three kings of O - ri - ent are;

bear - ing gifts we tra - verse a - far,

field and foun - tain, moor and moun - tain,

fol - low - ing yon - der star. O_____

star of won - der, star of night,

star   with   roy - al   beau - ty   bright,

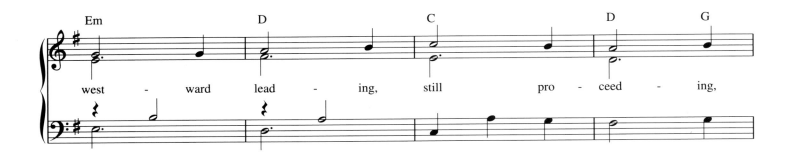

west - ward   lead - ing,   still   pro - ceed - ing,

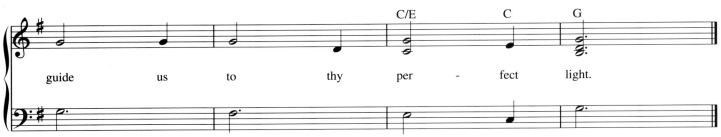

guide   us   to   thy   per - fect   light.

Copyright © 1992 by HAL LEONARD PUBLISHING CORPORATION
International Copyright Secured   All Rights Reserved

2. Born a King on Bethlehem's plain,
   Gold I bring, to crown Him again,
   King forever ceasing never
   Over us all to reign.

3. Frankincense to offer have I,
   Incense owns a Deity nigh.
   Pray'r and praising all men raising,
   Worship Him, God most high.

4. Myrrh is mine, its bitter perfume
   Breathes a life of gathering gloom;
   Sorr'wing, sighing, bleeding, dying,
   Sealed in the stone cold tomb.

5. Glorious now behold Him arise,
   King and God and Sacrifice,
   Alleluia, Alleluia,
   Earth to the heav'ns replies.

Nicolo da Urbino, active 1520s–c. 1537/1538
*Plaque with scene of the Adoration of the Magi,
in an extensive landscape* (c. 1525)

WHAT CHILD IS THIS?

Words by WILLIAM DIX
Traditional English Melody

1. What Child is this, _____ who, laid to rest, _____ On Mar - y's lap _____ is sleep - ing? Whom an - gels greet _____ with an - thems sweet _____ While shep - herds watch _____ are keep - ing? This, this _____ is Christ the King _____ Whom

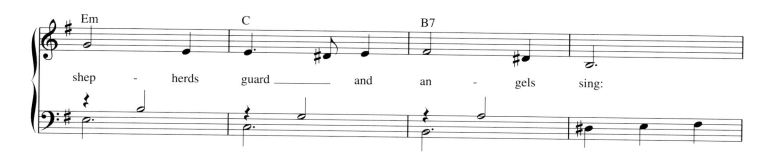

shep - herds guard _____ and an - gels sing:

Haste, haste _____ to bring Him laud _____ The

babe, _____ the Son _____ of Mar - y.

Copyright © 1992 by HAL LEONARD PUBLISHING CORPORATION
International Copyright Secured   All Rights Reserved

2. Why lies He in such mean estate,
   Where ox and ass are feeding?
   Good Christian, fear: for sinners here
   The silent Word is pleading.
   Nails, spear, shall pierce Him through,
   The Cross be borne, for me, for you:
   Hail, hail the Word made flesh,
   The Babe, the Son of Mary

3. So bring Him incense, gold and myrrh,
   Come peasant, king to own Him,
   The King of kings salvation brings,
   Let loving hearts enthrone Him.
   Raise, raise the song on high,
   The Virgin sings her lullaby:
   Joy, joy, for Christ is born,
   The Babe, the Son of Mary!

WHILE SHEPHERDS WATCHED THEIR FLOCKS BY NIGHT

Words by NAHUM TATE
Music by G.F. HANDEL

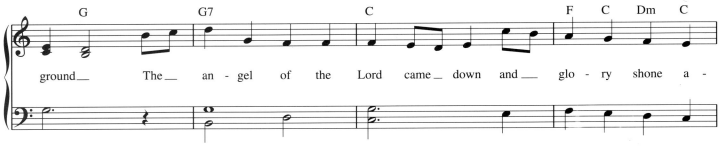

Copyright © 1992 by HAL LEONARD PUBLISHING CORPORATION
International Copyright Secured   All Rights Reserved

2. "Fear not!" said he for mighty dread
Had seized their troubled mind,
"Glad tidings of great joy I bring,
To you and all mankind,
To you and all mankind."

3. "To you, in David's town this day,
Is born of David's line,
The Savior who is Christ the Lord;
And this shall be the sign,
And this shall be the sign,"

4. "The heavenly Babe you there shall find
To human view displayed,
All meanly wrapped in swathing bands,
And in a manger laid,
And in a manger laid."

Jacopo Bassano, c. 1515–1592
The Annunciation to the Shepherds (probably c. 1555/1560)

LIST OF WORKS OF ART

All works of art reproduced in *Joy to the World: A Christmas Songbook* are in the permanent collection of the National Gallery of Art, Washington.

Fra Angelico, c. 1400–1455
and Fra Filippo Lippi, c. 1406–1469
The Adoration of the Magi (c. 1445)
tempera on wood
diameter: 1.372 m (54 in)
Samuel H. Kress Collection 1952.2.2

Hendrick Avercamp, 1585–1634
A Scene on the Ice (c. 1625)
oil on wood
0.393 x 0.771 m (15½ x 30⅜ in)
Ailsa Mellon Bruce Fund 1967.3.1

Jacopo Bassano, c. 1515–1592
The Annunciation to the Shepherds
(probably c. 1555/1560)
oil on canvas
1.061 x 0.826 m (41¾ x 32½ in)
Samuel H. Kress Collection 1939.1.126

Belbello de Pavia, active 1448/1462
Annunciation to the Virgin (1450/1460)
tempera and gold leaf on vellum
0.589 x 0.425 m (23⅛ x 16¾ in)
Rosenwald Collection 1948.11.21

Benvenuto di Giovanni, 1436–c. 1518
The Adoration of the Magi (c. 1470)
tempera on wood
1.823 x 1.375 m (71¾ x 54⅛ in)
Andrew W. Mellon Collection 1937.1.10

Hans Bol, 1534–1593
Winter Landscape with Skaters (c. 1584/1586)
pen and brown ink and wash on laid paper
0.193 x 0.269 m (7⁹⁄₁₆ x 10⁷⁄₁₆ in)
Gift of Robert H. and Clarice Smith, in Honor
of the 50th Anniversary of the National Gallery of Art
1991.15.1

Charles V. Bond, c. 1825-in or after 1864
Still Life: Fruit, Bird, and Dwarf Pear Tree (1856)
canvas
0.635 x 0.765 m (25 x 30⅛ in)
Gift of Edgar William and Bernice Chrysler Garbisch
1980.62.2

Botticelli, 1444/1445–1510
The Adoration of the Magi (early 1480s)
tempera on wood
0.702 x 1.042 m (27⅝ x 41 in)
Andrew W. Mellon Collection 1937.1.22

Rendered by Lucille Chabot, c. 1939
Gabriel Weather Vane (1840)
watercolor
0.362 x 0.524 m (14¼ x 20⅝ in)
Index of American Design 1943.8.9505
(MASS-me-19)

Thomas Cole, 1801–1848
The Voyage of Life: Youth (1842)
canvas
1.343 x 1.949 m (52⅞ x 76¾ in)
Ailsa Mellon Bruce Fund 1971.16.2

Lucas Cranach, the Elder, 1472–1553
Hunter on Horseback Hunting
a Wild Boar (c. 1506)
woodcut
0.179 x 0.122 m (7 x 4¹³⁄₁₆ in)
Rosenwald Collection 1943.3.2852

Gerard David, c. 1460–1523
The Rest on the Flight into Egypt (c. 1510)
oil on oak
painted surface: 0.419 x 0.422 m (16½ x 16⅝ in)
Andrew W. Mellon Collection 1937.1.43

Duccio di Buoninsegna, c. 1255–1318
Center Panel: *The Nativity with the Prophets Isaiah and*
Ezekiel (1308/1311)
wood
0.438 x 0.444 m (17¼ x 17½ in)
Andrew W. Mellon Collection 1937.1.8b

After Annibale Fontana
The Adoration of the Shepherds (c. 1625/1675)
terra cotta
1.090 x 0.570 m (43 x 22½ in)
Samuel H. Kress Collection 1939.1.319

Agnolo Gaddi, active 1369–1396
The Coronation of the Virgin (detail)
(probably c. 1370)
tempera on wood
1.626 x 0.794 m (64 x 31¼ in)
Samuel H. Kress Collection 1939.1.203

German, 15th Century
Madonna in a Closed Garden (1450/1470)
woodcut in brown, hand-colored in red lake,
yellow, green, gray, and tan
0.192 x 0.136 m (7½ x 5⅜ in)
Rosenwald Collection 1943.3.562

Rendered by Pearl Gibbo, c. 1935/1942
Santa Claus Print (1888)
watercolor
0.229 x 0.293 m (9 x 11⁹/₁₆ in)
Index of American Design 1943.8.869
(NYS-te-212)

Hendrik Goltzius, 1558–1617
*The Holy Family with Saint Elizabeth and Saint
John the Baptist* (1595)
pen and brown ink, brown wash, and white heightening
on brown laid paper
0.384 x 0.334 m (15⅛ x 13⅛ in)
Patrons' Permanent Fund 1989.19.1

Rendered by Charles Henning, c. 1940
Toy Bank: Santa Claus (c. 1940)
watercolor, gouache, and graphite on paperboard
0.289 x 0.222 m (11⅜ x 8¾ in)
Index of American Design 1943.8.8537
(NYC-me-i-351)

Rendered by Charles Henning, c. 1940
Toy Locomotive (1850–1875)
watercolor and graphite
0.375 x 0.485 m (14¾ x 19¹/₁₆ in)
Index of American Design 1943.8.13989
(NYC-mscl-toys-99)

Edward Hicks, 1780–1849
Peaceable Kingdom (c. 1834)
canvas
0.762 x 0.902 m (30 x 35½ in)
Gift of Edgar William and Bernice Chrysler Garbisch
1980.62.15

Adriaen Isenbrant, active 1510-1551
The Adoration of the Shepherds (probably 1520/1540)
oil on oak?
0.746 x 0.570 m (29⁷/₁₆ x 22⁷/₁₆ in)
Ailsa Mellon Bruce Fund 1978.46.1

Italian, 13th Century
The Nativity with Six Dominican Monks (c. 1275)
miniature on vellum
0.468 x 0.360 m (18½ x 14¼ in)
Rosenwald Collection 1946.21.12

Juan de Flandes, active 1496–1519
The Nativity (c. 1508/1519)
oil and tempera on wood
painted surface: 1.105 x 0.793 m (43½ x 31¼ in)
Samuel H. Kress Collection 1961.9.23

Lorenzo Lotto, c. 1480–1556
The Nativity (1523)
oil on wood
0.460 x 0.359 m (18⅛ x 14⅛ in)
Samuel H. Kress Collection 1939.1.288

Rendered by Mina Lowry, c. 1936
Top (c. 1830)
watercolor, graphite, and gouache on paper
0.286 x 0.222 m (11⅝ x 8⅝ in)
Index of American Design 1943.8.13990
(NYC-mscl-toys-20)

Rendered by Mina Lowry, c. 1937
Toy Horse (c. 1830)
watercolor, gouache, and graphite on paperboard
0.214 x 0.280 m (8⅜ x 11 in)
Index of American Design 1943.8.13992
(NYC-mscl-toys-67)

Master of the Cypresses, active 1434
Initial D (1430s)
miniature on vellum
0.170 x 0.215 m (6⅝ x 8½ in)
Rosenwald Collection 1964.8.1221

Master of the Cypresses, active 1434
Initial S with King David as Scribe (1430s)
miniature on vellum
0.176 x 0.173 m (6¹⁵⁄₁₆ x 6¹³⁄₁₆ in)
Rosenwald Collection 1964.8.1218

Master of the Dominican Effigies, active 1336/1345
*The Nativity with the Annunciation to
the Shepherds* (c. 1340)
miniature on vellum
0.365 x 0.271 m (14⁵⁄₁₆ x 10¹¹⁄₁₆ in)
Rosenwald Collection 1949.5.87

Claude Monet, 1840–1926
Rouen Cathedral, West Façade, Sunlight (1894)
oil on linen
1.002 x 0.660 m (39½ x 26 in)
Chester Dale Collection 1963.10.179

Benedetto Montagna, c. 1480–1555 or 1558
Shepherd with a Platerspiel (c. 1500/1515)
engraving
sheet (trimmed within plate mark): 0.097 x 0.076 m
(3¹³⁄₁₆ x 3 in)
Rosenwald Collection 1943.3.6247

Nicolo da Urbino, active 1520s–c. 1537/1538
*Plaque with scene of the Adoration of the Magi,
in an extensive landscape* (c. 1525)
earthenware (majolica)
0.222 x 0.165 m (8¾ x 6½ in)
Widener Collection 1942.9.341

Frances Flora Bond Palmer, c. 1812–1876
American Winter Scenes: Morning (published 1854)
hand-colored lithograph on wove paper
image: 0.415 x 0.609 m (16⅜ x 23¹⁵⁄₁₆ in)
Collection of Mr. and Mrs. Paul Mellon 1985.64.158

Samuel Palmer, 1805–1881
The Sleeping Shepherd; Early Morning (1857)
etching, hand-colored with watercolor and opaque
white with gold highlights
plate: 0.095 x 0.078 m (3¾ x 3¹⁄₁₆ in)
Rosenwald Collection 1943.3.6711

Rendered by Esther Peck, c. 1935/1942
Doll (1867)
watercolor and graphite with heightening
0.292 x 0.229 m (11½ x 8¹⁵⁄₁₆ in)
Index of American Design 1943.8.13991
(NYC-mscl-toys-61)

Raphael, 1483–1520
The Small Cowper Madonna (c. 1505)
oil on wood
0.595 x 0.440 m (23⅜ x 17⅜ in)
Widener Collection 1942.9.57

Rendered by Michael Riccitelli, c. 1939
Carousel Reindeer (c. 1890)
watercolor, graphite, and colored pencil on paperboard
0.362 x 0.490 m (14¼ x 19¼ in)
Index of American Design 1943.8.8025
(RI-ca-130)

Andrea della Robbia, 1435–1525
The Adoration of the Child (after 1477)
terra cotta, glazed
1.278 x 0.774 m (50⅜ x 30½ in)
Samuel H. Kress Collection 1961.1.2

Robert Salmon, 1775–c. 1845
The Ship "Favorite" Maneuvering off Greenock (1819)
canvas
0.762 x 1.283 m (30 x 50½ in)
Paul Mellon Collection 1981.54.1

Martin Schongauer, c. 1450–1491
Madonna on the Crescent (c. 1470)
engraving
0.172 x 0.108 m (6¾ x 4¼ in)
Rosenwald Collection 1943.3.50

Martin Schongauer, c. 1450–1491
The Nativity (c. 1470/1475)
engraving
0.254 x 0.168 m (10 x 6⅝ in)
Rosenwald Collection 1943.3.29

Martin Schongauer, c. 1450–1491
The Nativity (c. 1480/1490)
engraving
0.160 x 0.153 m (6¼ x 6¹⁄₁₆ in)
Rosenwald Collection 1944.2.72

Jan Steen, 1626–1679
The Dancing Couple (1663)
canvas
1.025 x 1.425 m (40⅜ x 56⅛ in)
Widener Collection 1942.9.81

David Teniers II, 1610–1690
Peasants Celebrating Twelfth Night (1635)
oil on wood
0.472 x 0.699 m (18⅝ x 27½ in)
Ailsa Mellon Bruce Fund 1972.10.1

Jacopo Tintoretto, 1518–1594
The Madonna of the Stars (second half 16th century)
oil on canvas
0.927 x 0.727 m (36½ x 28⅝ in)
Ralph and Mary Booth Collection 1947.6.6

INDEX OF SONGS